C

DEPENDENCE

An

A-> Z

A Dictionary of...
...Codependence

By Rob M

An A to Z of Co-Dependence

Rob M asserts his right to be credited as the author of this work.

Thanks...

Thanks are of course due to many people. Apologies are due to even more...

A bit about the Author...

After reaching almost 60 years old and almost completely failing to grow up, I was introduced to CoDA** in 2006. I received an ultimatum; "Go to CoDA and stop being so co-dependent. Or stop seeing me!"

I had previously concluded (after three failed marriages) that I was genetically flawed, so I felt enormous relief in finding, at CoDA meetings, that I was potentially fixable. I was reluctant to put it to the test however.

After four years of going to meetings I (reluctantly) started on the steps. After four more years I began work on this booklet. And, after

2

being stuck on "Procrastination" for another seven years, I finished it.

Since starting with CoDA I have served as a town councillor and done numerous other things that were previously unthinkable. I now feel fairly comfortable with life. I no longer live in fear. And it is all down to CoDA – and "my" Higher Power of course.

I can even say that I seem to have grown up bit, I can ask questions, I can keep confidences, I can say "No" when I want to say no. I regard rescuing as interfering in people's lives. But there is still plenty of room for improvement.

Note: Yes, one could indeed write a whole book about any one of these topics. And many people have done so. There are plenty of books on codependence out there already, so this is just a quick rundown of what I have learned over the last few years… Feel free to add your take on things. Email me on dinger493@gmail.com.

** CoDA: Codependents Anonymous. A 12 step program of recovery from co-dependency.

An A to Z of Co-Dependence

Based on the 12 steps of Alcoholics Anonymous.

Note: In accordance with the tradition of anonymity in 12 step groups, Rob M declines to reveal his full name.

A word of Caution

If anything in this book begins to affect you adversely, please seek help. This book does not attempt to offer solutions. Merely to raise red flags – and point you to CoDA perhaps.

Introduction

Many of us grew up with various ideas about life that have ultimately proven to be unproductive and often profoundly damaging, to ourselves and others - particularly in adult life. These ideas can actually prevent us from properly making the transition into adulthood, thus our behaviours and responses (reactions) remain childish.

The following behaviour patterns, when indulged in, appear to keep us in "child mode". I have found that a good part of my recovery has been down to my being made aware of my childish behaviours, and by gradually letting go of them I have been able to begin the transition to adulthood.

Other activities that have helped me are going to meetings of Co-dependents Anonymous, working the program (12 steps). Doing "Service work". I.e. chairing meetings, holding posts such as Treasurer, Secretary etc.

An A to Z of Co-Dependence

By speaking at meetings I began to find my voice. I gradually learned to express my opinion in an adult way. I slowly learned to interrogate my own feelings. By attending meetings I learned that others had similar issues. I learned to care about them too - not just about me.

After a few years in recovery you may be asked to "sponsor" others (act as a mentor). This is another very powerful way to enhance recovery. The sponsor usually gets more out of the process than the sponsee!

It appears that as children we adopt behaviours designed to enhance our survival prospects. We set out to manipulate our care givers into enabling this. We need food, shelter, and love (attention). We set out to get this with any means at our disposal. We need to get attention. Sometimes this means being good, sometimes bad. Some of us try to become invisible, some shine at school but misbehave at home. There is much written on the subject (I was invisible).

An A to Z of Co-Dependence

The idea is however, that some of these behaviours become so ingrained that we cannot let them go when it is time to become independent. We remain dependent on others and fail to mature into properly functioning adults, with consequent relationship issues. This is what Coda seeks to address.

A properly functioning adult will not (usually) seek a relationship with a co-dependent (or otherwise dysfunctional) person, thus co-dependents will usually find themselves in relationship with another co-dependent - each seeking to be dependent on the other. Sounds like a recipe for disaster? It is!

If you find yourself attracted to a person who is a bit of a fruit cake, ask yourself, "Why am I attracted to this person?" Is it because you see them as vulnerable? Are you seeking to take advantage of them in some way? Are you a fruit cake too?

There are many other dysfunctional personality types that will attempt to form relationships with co-dependents, but that is not within the scope of this book. (Those relationships are no more successful of course)

If you think that the above sounds like nearly everybody you know, then I have to agree. But this not about them, it's about YOU! Are <u>you</u> satisfied with the way *your* life is? Are you satisfied with your relationships? If not then perhaps Coda is for you. But, a word of caution - when only one person in a co-dependent relationship starts in recovery, the other will usually feel threatened and oppose any changes, pulling the partner back into the dysfunctional relationship even harder.. .

A breakup is the usual result.

An A to Z of Co-Dependence

Get these ideas into your head:

1. People Pleasing means being a doormat
2. Being a doormat means having no self-esteem
3. No self-esteem means staying repressed and depressed, all your life
4. Rescuing means Interfering in other's lives
5. Advice giving (unasked for) is telling others that they are useless
6. Caretaking others means not having a life yourself
7. Being over Helpful means not having an identity of your own
8. No Identity means no Values of your own
9. No Values means no Boundaries
10. No Boundaries means your life is not your own
11. All of this means you won't be able to grow up - your childhood programming will always dominate you.
12. There is a way forward: Get to a MEETING and stop being so co-dependent!

An A to Z of Co-Dependence

It is purely coincidental that there are 12 items listed above. These are <u>not</u> the 12 steps.

An A to Z of Co-Dependence

CONTENTS

An A to Z of Co-Dependence

An A to Z of Co-Dependence

An A to Z of Co-Dependence

An A to Z of Co-Dependence

An A to Z of Co-Dependence

An A to Z of Co-Dependence

Abandonment

This chapter would have to come first, even if Aardvark was a Co-dependent trait. It's that fundamental to understanding the roots of co-dependence.

Abandonment can be Physical or Emotional or both. This is what the child fears most. It means death. Certain death (a child cannot find food or shelter by itself). A child in constant fear of certain death will almost certainly have big trouble later in life. Letting go of that fear and embracing life will probably be a whole life's work. Until the child can begin to let go of the fear he/she will be relatively unable to move into adulthood. They may never grow up properly, always reacting from child and only having half a life. A life filled with anxiety, depression, addictions, shame and fear.

A well-documented phenomenon is that of the Adult-Child-of-Alcoholic (ACOA). One or both parents may be alcoholic. Inevitably the child will receive mixed messages. A loving parent can suddenly become abusive. A parent may promise the earth but never deliver. There is much literature on the subject. The child will probably become dysfunctional and is likely to become alcoholic themselves. There are many traits that characterise such a child. These traits can be observed in children whose parents were not alcoholic however. These parents probably had other dysfunctions that affected their ability to parent effectively. Perhaps they had other mental illnesses, or non-substance addictions such as workaholism. So I conclude that it is not the parental alcoholism per se that produces the dysfunctional child, but the dysfunctional parental behaviours. Thus any child deprived of a secure upbringing, either through lack of adequate role modelling, lack of wider family support etc. may exhibit dysfunctional traits that may well need psychiatric attention in the future.

A cause for concern should also be the very well behaved child. This child could well be afraid of losing what little support he has, so attempts to manipulate the care givers into liking, and thus caring for, him more, thus enabling him to survive. More secure children will push the boundaries, enabling them to grow and adapt to the world, whilst they are sure of parental support. This pushing of boundaries could be seen as being naughty of course. Paradoxically, naughty children could be "good" children (and have good parents) and vice versa! There will always be exceptions to this "rule" of course. Alternatively a child may be rebelling against excessively controlling or unsupportive parents with whom no amount of good behaviour gets good results. That is why they have changed, or adopted, different tactics. The goal is the same; to get attention and support.

The abandoned child never received the unconditional parental love that every child craves. He or she will spend eternity looking for that love. It will get them into all sorts of unsuitable relationships (with similarly abandoned children). The relationships will be characterised by addictions, violence, divorce and poverty - and the dis-ease will be passed on to their children. The dysfunction does not appear to dissipate. It appears to become more acute with each generation.

See: Generational Dysfunction.

Abuse

It appears to be a general observation that almost all abuse is perpetrated by individuals trying to "get their needs met". They are likely to be "stuck in child" and live in fear of abandonment. These people have a low level of awareness generally, and are likely not significantly aware of their behaviours towards others, or of other people as persons separate from themselves.

There are almost certainly exceptions to this generalisation. These persons may be more seriously damaged - being psychopaths or whatever.

Forms abuse can take:

An A to Z of Co-Dependence

- Ignoring someone
- Denying another's truth
- Blackmail / threats
- Withdrawing love / passive aggressive behaviour
- Inconsistency
- Talking over someone
- Belittling
- Using one's authority / abuse of power / bullying
- Taking over a task or conversation (undermining)
- False accusations
- Gas-lighting
- Constant staring – controlling
- Talking incessantly

A Co-dependent will often ignore being ignored. They will rationalise it by saying to themselves; "They didn't see/hear me" or "they hadn't got their glasses/hearing aid". Whilst these may be true we must be careful not to allow people to treat us badly, or take us for granted. It becomes accepted as normal, and it has negative effects on our self-esteem.

An A to Z of Co-Dependence

Be careful not to minimise the importance of how someone else feels. Simply telling them to "pull your-self together" and refuse to hear what they are trying to communicate is disrespectful of them. Try to really hear what they are saying.

A person may use threats in order to get what they want. This can result in violence of course. The threat is of course designed to trigger "our stuff", thus putting us into "victim". This is an opportunity for growth. Take it to your sponsor and work through it.

Withdrawing of any kind is known as "passive aggressive". See it for what it is and try to open a dialogue. The person will need lots of reassurance in order to overcome the fear (of abandonment) that is (probably) driving the behaviour.

When a person says one thing, then does another, this is likely to be a way of keeping control. The other person never knows where they stand and is constantly playing "catch-up". This is designed to make a person feel crazy, especially as it is usually accompanied by total denial on the part of the perpetrator. This is Gas-Lighting. This person is a really nasty (sad and frightened) person, bordering on psychopathic.

And perhaps....drunk on power - therapists can't help them - and <u>neither can you</u>. Get out of there!

Talking over others is the mark of a narcissist. If they do allow you to speak, they won't hear what you say. They will just bring the "conversation" (it's not one) back around to themselves as quickly as they can. They can be fun to be with, but ultimately they are abusers. And they will bring you down.

Being made to feel less-than, stupid, or not good enough. It's what many of us suffered as children, whether from parents or teachers. We grew up feeling ashamed of who we were - and responsible for the disappointment our care-givers felt in us. Don't allow it to happen again, and don't do it to others. Keep away from those who do it, and try to build up those you have contact with.

An A to Z of Co-Dependence

When someone uses their authority over you to get what they want, it undermines your very identity and personhood. You are being treated as less of a human than they are. Whether it be because of their status, wealth, colour or sex - it is unacceptable.

When someone takes over from you, if they see you having difficulty, they are really saying (sub-text) that you are "incompetent" at the very least. Don't let them do it. And be careful not to do it to others.

People who falsely accuse others are likely guilty of that very thing themselves. They are in denial, and are very sick people.

Gas-Lighting refers to a film wherein the villain denied the realty of his victim's perceptions, thus undermining her grip on sanity. The victim thus becomes utterly unable to function. The modern crime of Coercive Control seems close-ly related to this form of abuse.

Constant staring can be seen as abusive. The perpetrator is exercising a form of control. Be aware of your surroundings and what you, and others, are doing.

Acceptance

Acceptance of what is - of what we cannot change. This does not mean allowing any abusive behaviour towards us to continue - we must seek help if necessary, once it has been recognized for what it is.

What is helpful to come to acceptance about could include:

The different ways others do things. If they choose to do things in a less effective way than you do, then that is their choice. Allow them their power.

Friends/siblings/spouse behaving in an embarrassing way - well you may just have to let them! Beware of behaving in a passive-aggressive or controlling way, in your attempts to avoid your own embarrassed feelings. You probably have the right to advise your non-adult offspring, that you disapprove of their behaviours, however. Beware also of any enabling you may be tempted to do, such as clearing up a spouse's vomit (assuming result of self-inflicted drunkenness) or even just clearing up after a party when they are sleeping it off (been there...). I know it's difficult to leave a mess when animals and children are liable to tread it all over the house.

Many of us are concerned about social issues, climate change, politics, corruption etc. This can really affect those of us who became over-responsible for others in their childhood, those of us who were made to feel it was "their fault" - we came to feel a lot of guilt and shame. In adulthood we came to believe we were responsible for "saving the world", supporting causes, contributing as much as we could, knowing that it was never enough, rescuing animals, spreading the word to friends and colleagues, fund raising , delivering leaflets for charities, political parties - you name them, there are more causes than ever, and all seemingly worthwhile. . But it is not all down to *us*, we can allow others to do their part - we cannot do it alone, and in fact it will not be noticeably affected by our contribution or lack thereof. We *are* allowed to take time out and smell the roses - if not the coffee! We can (and must) let go of the feeling that we are responsible. We must put *our* needs, and the needs of *our* families, first.

Make a list of what concerns you: (here's my list)

- climate Change
- Pollution
- Refugee crisis
- Species loss
- Corruption
- Resource Depletion etc.

How worried are you personally? Are <u>you</u> feeling that <u>you</u> should be doing more to raise awareness or change your own carbon footprint for example? There are things you can do, but make sure you allow yourself some fun times too.

People behaving anti-socially makes me very cross

- Aggressive driving
- Noisy Neighbours / vehicles
- Dropping litter
- Allowing dogs to foul

Don't get angry (don't react from child). If you need to respond, try and find a non-confrontational form of words: "Did you forget the poop bags?" Otherwise you may need to accept that they are perhaps in a less aware place, or maybe have issues you are unaware of. Don't make their problems into your problems. Let it go. If you do begin to obsess about it, try and imagine how it could have gone, if you had found some adult form of words to say. (think of some) Rehearse some adult conversations in your head (with yourself).

Addictions

An A to Z of Co-Dependence

Addiction - to anything - is more than likely an obsessive compulsive phenomenon. As such it is therefore an avoidance act. We are seeking to avoid personal responsibility yet again. Avoiding facing our fears, our responsibility towards ourselves, our self-defeating beliefs. We don't want to change, because we believe we will fail - and then we will really be in the mire, having proved we cannot change. We would rather hide ourselves away than face our demons. Yet if we look closely at them we usually find that they are not as big and bad as we feared. This is where going to meetings is so helpful. We find that others have the same fears as us - and they can talk about them. Bringing them into the open, into the cold light of day, destroys their power over us.

Addiction triggers the reward pathways in the brain. We can get deeply locked into this pattern of behaviour. But! You can break the cycle. It may take years but it must be done. Find other enjoyable, but non-addictive activities that you can substitute for destructive addictive activities, which deep down, you are ashamed of!

Every time you stop indulging in your addiction, you undo a bit of the power of it over you.

Addiction doesn't have to be to a substance. It can be a behaviour, such as indulging in fantasies, gambling and pornography. All of these things destroy our abilities to grow into fully functioning adults with a rich inner life, and have meaningful relationships with others.

Advice Giving

Giving advice. Were you asked to give it? If so then it may be okay, but limit what you say and be careful how you say it.

Un-asked for advice is really (sub-text) telling the other person that they are inadequate in some way, deficient in knowledge or expertise. Don't be surprised if they become resentful.

These days I often say "I have no idea" even when I have a very good idea! Particularly when it is well within the capability of the other person to find out for themselves, from the Internet or wherever. They are thus empowered, and I am not risking dis-empowering them.

Do not do for others what they can do for themselves!

Answers - Having them All

When asked for an opinion or an answer do you automatically give a 'best guess'? (And pass it off as fact?).
Are you in fact, unable to say: "I don't know"?

Well, that was me. I think that maybe, somewhere in the past, probably (definitely) school, I was punished, belittled, berated and humiliated, for not knowing some totally irrelevant nonsense. So I became compelled to give answers - to everyone, about anything!

I now find it very liberating to say "I don't know" - even if I do. "I have no idea" I say (Let them find out for themselves). Not my problem I say (to myself), unless it is of course. I do still help whenever I can (when asked).

Attachment

"Attachment" is generally seen as being the attachment of the child to its parent(s).

In Coda we are thinking in terms of "addiction" (to people, places and things) and "dependency". As a child we are normally attached to, and dependent on, our mother. We would normally grow up and become independent from our parents and become interdependent with other young adults. Co-dependency appears to be swapping the parent-child attachment phase for a mutually dependent phase with another child-adult - and all but halting the "growing up" phase.

Attention seeking

If someone's behaviour is perplexing you, ask yourself "What are they getting out of it?" Maybe they are just looking for attention!

It could be feigning illness, or similar. It will usually be something that means they need rescuing, or help. But see "Victimhood".

You could be sympathetic and try and help them get to the bottom of their problem. But they won't thank you for it. You are just giving them the attention they need. They won't act on your suggestions. Leave them to the professionals!

If their behaviour is actually causing you a problem, you may have to do some empathetic listening.

Assuming

Or: **Making Assumptions**. Assuming that you know how others feel, assuming that you know what they want, assuming that you know best, assuming that others want to hear all about you - or your holiday.

You don't know anything at all! So let them be.

You may **_think_** you know how they feel, or what they want, but do you really? Have you asked them, have you allowed them to tell you?

Avoidance

We may be avoiding responsibility for our own lives, we may be avoiding feeling our own feelings. We may be chronic procrastinators, hoarders, caretakers and rescuers. Addicts of all kinds. But see; Addiction, Feelings and Procrastination.

Boundaries

Until you have found out who you are, defined yourself, built or re-built your identity, you will not be able to define healthy boundaries - as there is little or nothing to put boundaries around. So go and read the sections on identity then come back and finish this section.

Boundaries are definitions of what you will and will not accept in the behaviour of others towards you. People with strong boundaries will react strongly to boundary violations. Codependents will take huge amounts of abuse in order to avoid the risk of being disliked. And of course that is the result anyway.

Caretaking

We become caretakers through our childhood training. We are given the job of looking after an elderly relative or a dysfunctional parent or even younger siblings. We are told that we must do this to be a good person. If we don't do this then we are a bad person.

We are thus made to feel that we are responsible for the well-being of the other people around us - otherwise we are a bad person.

Even when the initial responsibility stops, when we leave home or whatever, we continue to look out for the needs of those around us. We are now programmed to do this. We ignore our own needs.

We continue to be afraid of being labelled as a "bad person".

Catastrophising

See Negativity.

Dwelling on negative outcomes, always looking for negative motives or reasons for events - when more benign reasons could be found. For instance, I read recently (on a Catastrophising website) that a "reversal of the Earth's magnetic field is imminent", and that this will "probably wipe out life on Earth". Instead of repeating this information verbatim, it is well to reflect that the Earth's magnetic field actually moves around all the time and will probably continue to oscillate as normal, and nothing much will happen for a very long time. We must avoid jumping to conclusions and making assumptions. Sometimes we like to be the bearers of bad news - it makes us feel important in our own eyes. Bear in mind that it may make us look childish in others' eyes.

Childish Behaviours

Not doing as you're told. That is, not obeying the voice of authority/common sense. For me this is very likely an attempt at self-sabotage. I resent authority and attempt to destroy it in a passive-aggressive kind of way - by just not doing *exactly* as I'm told.

Many times I have come unstuck with this behaviour. Things have gone wrong or work has had to be rectified because I didn't do exactly as I was told. I was then to blame, but inside I did not accept the responsibility. Thus I am stuck in "child" and never grew up into a responsible adult.

Just lately I have gone back to sailing. This time on a larger boat, crewing for the owner. The owner is dependent on me being there to crew for him. I am dependent on him as the boat owner, to pay for the running costs etc. It became obvious to me quite soon that for safety's sake I had to do exactly as I was told on the boat. It was his boat, his responsibility. No place for acting out on resentments. I could not afford to be responsible for any mishaps. Any mishaps had to be down to someone/something else. (I began to grow up!)

I could still give my opinion of course, if there was a debate as to best course of action, which I did - a bit too much I think. As crew my tasks involved mooring up to quaysides and casting off buoys etc. When the owner expressed concerns about a particularly tricky situation (other boats in the way, winds, tides etc. against us) I would give him detailed instructions as to the way forward (in my opinion). But it always went wrong. He could never do exactly as I said. He was sabotaging me! He was resenting me telling him what to do, and going into "child" himself, did something else. Now that I understand what is going wrong I can step back and let him make the decisions.

Confrontation

Most co-dependents will avoid confrontation like the plague. It must trigger some deep seated fears from childhood. This means that things like returning faulty goods to a shop or complaining in a restaurant are really frightening things to have to do. Co-dependents just can't do those things (and feel comfortable) in an adult way.

I have found that taking the time to get clear in my head what it is that I wish to say, and running through the likely conversation (again, in my head) beforehand helps a lot. (see: <u>Letting go of outcomes</u>)

Finding the right form of words is not easy, since as co-dependents we have not got an adult vocabulary.
See: <u>Keep it to you</u>

Take the time to remember how you were treated by authority figures as a child. Were you humiliated, shamed, ignored, shouted at, bullied, hit even? Any one of these things will cause you to fear confrontation.

Don't shy away from any feelings that come up. Let them come, cry a little. Realise that it is the child in you who is hurting. Comfort him/her.

Controlling Others

I thought that the last thing I was, was Controlling. But I discovered that Controlling takes many forms.

An A to Z of Co-Dependence

Why do we control? Essentially it appears to me that we control others to keep ourselves safe. Which self? The adult or child within? A fully realised Adult will not generally be power-less or allow others to take his power and will thus feel safe around other people. The "Child" however will react to its programming - and do whatever is necessary to ensure its survival. If the inner child has primacy over the adult then it will assert its coping mechanisms. Thus the adult will behave as a child.

As an infant we were of course totally depend-ent on our care givers for our survival. It is as basic as that. Even today's welfare state regu-larly fails to protect children from uncaring parents. Thus the child learns very quickly who its care givers are and how to manipulate them into meeting its needs. A quick smile here, a giggle or a cry, brings instant reaction - and succour. Later this becomes more sophisticat-ed and each sibling can take a specific role in holding a dysfunctional family together long enough to ensure their survival. These roles then have to be unlearnt and discarded in the process of moving into adulthood. If these childhood reactions are retained the result will be a dysfunctional and unhappy adult-child.

The adult-child will be ill at ease with themselves and others and may well deal with their discomfort via compulsions, fantasy life, addictions etc.

Some Control Tactics

1. Intimidation, threats to leave, commit suicide etc.
2. Undermining the other, by criticism, ridicule, exposing incompetence (rescuing)
3. Withdrawing - silences, sulking, non-cooperation (passive-aggressive).
4. Playing the Victim. Getting attention, thus control. The victim can then legitimately go into Persecutor..
5. Lending books, DVDs, the inference being "I know more than you"
6. Twisting words, taking words out of context
7. Gossip to others about you, so that they are biased against you...

8. Holding on to past misdemeanours and bring them up years after they have ceased to be relevant
9. Lying, and insisting it is your memory that is at fault - undermining again
10. Accusations of lying, infidelity, cheating - the irony here is that the accuser is often guilty of all the things they accuse the other of.
11. Giving unwanted advice - again the inference is that the other is incompetent...
12. Any attention seeking activity can be seen as controlling.

As can be readily appreciated, almost all of the above can readily be observed in children. QED. They are childish behaviours. My score? (6/12).

Damage done to One-self / Others

An A to Z of Co-Dependence

The harm done through co-dependent behaviours can be divided into damage to one's self and damage to others. Both kinds are detrimental to healthy relationships of course.

If I do not act as an adult, then I do not keep the respect of colleagues, spouse or offspring, siblings etc.

1. At work I will fail to gain promotion, I will not achieve targets etc. Earning power is reduced.
2. My spouse will not respect me. I will fail to meet his/her needs/expectations. Relationship will be poor quality and short lived in all likelihood.
3. My offspring will not receive healthy role modelling - with consequent problems to themselves - addictions, unruly behaviours, poor prospects.
4. My siblings will have a low opinion of me and be distant and unsupportive.
5. Elderly parents will perhaps worry themselves into an early grave.

6. Any friendships are likely to be with similarly dysfunctional people - healthy people will not find me interesting or fun to be with.

Recognising my childish behaviours helps me to stop doing them and to grow up bit by bit. As a co-dependent I have been acting "as if" for a long time. It is hard work, debilitating - and false. And it doesn't actually help one to grow up much.

If I hold on to co-dependent behaviours then:

7. I fail to transition to adulthood
8. I hold on to childish behaviours
9. I fail to develop an adult identity
10. I am unlikely to have satisfactory relationships
11. My self-esteem will be low
12. My awareness of others is low
13. My awareness of my own needs is low
14. My self-confidence is low
15. My ability to make decisions is poor
16. My awareness of the world around me is low

17. My thinking is very reactionary/second hand opinions
18. My judgment is poor
19. I am easily swayed and taken in by stronger personalities
20. I am easily taken in by persuasive advertising etc.
21. My financial decisions will be poor

This is because Co-dependents:

22. Identity is dependent on others around them
23. Awareness of self is low
24. Awareness of personal boundaries and consequent violations is low
25. Are essentially children
26. Opinions are dependent on the opinions of others around them
27. Values are similarly dependent on others
28. Are not aware of own or others needs
29. Are not aware of own or others feelings
30. Are not aware of own or others boundaries
31. Are not aware of their own childishness

32. Are not aware of how they affect other people
33. Are not aware of the sub-texts of what they say
34. Are so consumed with others that they have no energy for themselves or what is really important
35. Are irresponsible

So what are our possible Childish behaviours?

36. Being afraid of life. We learned to fear the violence, anger, ridicule or criticism of our primary care-givers, our teachers, those in authority over us. We had no power, no choices. Some of us did rebel. They paid the price of missing out on their education by getting expelled - and/or left their families of origin completely. They kept their self-esteem however, and gained an identity perhaps. Realise that you do have the power now - if you can stop giving it away. You do have choices - if you can let go of the fear of authority.

37. Bad manners. Be aware of what you are doing and how others might perceive

your behaviours. Do not speak with your mouth full, eat with your mouth open or wave knives and forks around when you speak (guilty of all charges m'lud)

38. Sneezing loudly - I used to think it was funny - it's not - it's childish attention seeking. Ditto yawning loudly with mouth open.

39. Overeating. Cleaning up other people's left overs. For me this was probably because "mummy" was pleased with me when I ate up my dinner. I always ate what she had prepared. Be aware that your inner child is probably perceiving your dinner companion as "mother". She's not. Try and imagine how she might perceive your actions if you keep pigging-out. That is the route to change. Don't just "pretend" because I am suggesting it here. You have to put some effort in to understanding why you behave as you do. It was a way of getting mummy's attention. Possibly her love was perceived as conditional.

40. Not keeping confidences. We think we are important because we "know" some-

thing, so we spill the beans. Just shut up and listen. Maybe you will learn something important. Keep confidences to yourself.

41. Shouting down the street to your friends. This is just so uncouth - and intimidating for older people. Doing it at 3am and waking up an entire neighbourhood is just beyond the pale.

42. Thinking it is funny to be disrespectful of older people - so maybe you are angry at how you were treated? (as a child) Deal with it. Don't take it out on innocent vulnerable older people. That is just bullying.

43. Talking over other people. We need to respect what other people are saying. We should then respond to them, not ignore what they said and just say what we want to say.

44. Turning up unannounced. This is what teenagers do. Mummy never told us off (she was just so relieved to see us home again safely!) We need to respect other people's space/boundaries/time.

45. Playing stereo loudly in house or car, annoying neighbours / passers- by. Again childish attention seeking. Other people will not admire our choice of music!

46. We give our power to stronger (more grown up) people around us - seeing them as "Parent" figures and behave childishly.

47. Not looking after ourselves. Mummy is not going to remind us, or do it all for us, any more. It is up to us to clean up after ourselves, to wash, to clean our teeth, dress properly, eat and drink sensibly. Get to work on time, do what is required of you - and GET A LIFE!

Denial

This is NOT just a river in Egypt!

Denial, denial of the truth, in whatever form it appears. Denial of your own behaviour, denial of someone else's. Denial of problems that must be addressed, such as loss of a job or accommodation. Denial of symptoms of illness, making the time to recovery longer - or worse. Denial of the deterioration of a relationship, leading to prolonged agony for everyone.

Why do we do it? It must be fear. Fear that if we look too closely we will find that the situation is even worse than it might look right now. Fear that we are to blame, or will be blamed. Fear that the situation cannot be resolved, so we cling onto the last vestiges of what little comfort we have left.

In all cases being open to the truth will be healing. You will find support. But first we must let go of the fear. Ask for help, from your Higher Power or your sponsor, or from other agencies. You probably fear being refused help. You may not get it at your first attempt but remember, this is an exercise in accepting the truth. The truth about who you really are.

Devaluing Others

An A to Z of Co-Dependence

I will give a specific example here, then maybe we can come up with some general principles...

My girlfriend and I were out for a Sunday drive (I was driving) and she announced that she was "feeling a bit depressed". I reacted in my usual (co-dependent) way (instead of *Responding*) by saying "Oh, there's people much worse off than you" (which is sometimes ok). She responded crossly saying not to "devalue" her feelings. The sub-text of my response had been that "her feelings were wrong". If I had thought a bit harder and said something like "what has made you feel like that?" or "shall we stop and talk?" I might have gone up in her estimation instead of almost getting my marching orders.

My excuse was that I was driving, and having deep conversations whilst negotiating country lanes in Devon is tricky sometimes. The truth is that I was a co-dependent and this was my normal reaction to this kind of statement – driving or not.

I didn't want to start talking about feelings at all, hers or mine. It only opens a can of worms,

53

best to stuff it back under the carpet where it belongs...

So the upshot of the tale is that one should engage brain before opening mouth (and inserting foot).

Dogmatism

Being dogmatic must come from the attitude that "I am right", and "I have all the answers" and "you are therefore an ignoramus, and should accord me the deference due to my superior knowledge and wisdom!"

This must be highly annoying for those on the receiving end, and will likely lead to great resentments, you being ignored and having few friends.

Always try to preface your erudition with "I believe" or "it seems to me that...", "I would have said..." Or "perhaps...".

And even end with "...and what do you think?"

I like to say "I have no idea" these days, even when I have a very good idea!

Do's and Don'ts

These items will probably be explained more fully elsewhere in this document.

Don't explain yourself – unless you really are six years old.
Don't apologise (for being you) -unless necessary of course
Don't try and fix other people's feelings – just let them be.
Don't try and fix your own feelings - just stay with them.
Don't overindulge - in anything, food/drink/sex/shopping/drugs/sensations.
Don't assume anything.
Don't neglect yourself.
Don't take things personally.
Don't be attached to outcomes.

An A to Z of Co-Dependence

Don't dismiss others' feelings or needs as unimportant.
Don't indulge in distracting behaviour.
Don't fantasise.
Don't be irresponsible.
Don't be late.
Don't procrastinate.
Don't project, catastrophise, dwell on the negative, etc.
and don't take things too seriously!

Do:
Meditate, exercise, rest, eat healthily,
Keep in touch with your Higher Power – and your Sponsor
Take care of yourself, your appearance, your cleanliness, your clothing.
Take care of your surroundings - be comfortable and warm.
Take care of your money, pay your bills, be responsible - don't expect others to take care of you.
Respect others, their time, their money, their feelings, their property.
Get to appointments on time - let people know if you're going to be late or can't get there.

Go to Meetings - and do service!
Engage in life-long education, read, take classes, online courses,
Engage in social activities.
Take an interest in life - the sciences, the arts, politics, the economy, practical and social skills. People above all.
Watch what you say and what you do (unless you are perfect). It gives away your real motives.
Be aware of those around you. They give themselves away too, with what they say and what they do. Observe.
Be generous and forgiving. Understand that others may not be as aware as you are.
Be understanding and compassionate when others are unintentionally confrontational or are taking things personally.
Understand that we are all on different parts of the same path. It is not our place to judge.
Be positive above all.

Drama Triangle

An A to Z of Co-Dependence

Oddly this triangle only requires two persons. Any more and you probably have multiple triangles! (or squares)

This appears to be a compulsive "game" for two. Person A adopts a victim role, and invites person B to rescue him/her. Person A then becomes resentful of being lectured at and begins to attack person B, person A becoming the "persecutor". Person B then becomes a Victim. Person B can then become mired in "victim" until they become resentful and go into "Persecutor" themselves.

This is most obvious in an addiction scenario. Take an alcoholic. Usually he will be in "poor me" mode at some point (victim). This invites his enabler (usually wife) to rescue him by getting him another bottle of his poison. The alcoholic then resents being obligated and/or controlled by the rescuer and causes a scene, fight or row. Usually all three. Thus he is now the persecutor. The poor wife is now a victim of the alcoholic and probably feels guilty of all the accusations thrown at her. She may even go and get the alcoholic more hooch at this point to assuage her own guilt.

The only way to avoid this is to not respond at all to the first moves of the alcoholic. This is "tough love". Just get out of the house, and stay out. Once on the drama triangle the only way off is to walk away. Any reacting, arguments, threats etc. are just part of the drama. Shut up and leave (take the children with you).

Enabling

In the classic case the enabler enables the addict to continue in his addiction.
The enabler usually complies with the addicts demands in order to avoid the bad behaviours that result if they don't comply. Anything for a quiet life.

Their compliance usually starts off in a small way but before long they are breaking the law themselves to obtain drugs! You have been warned! Don't start!

But! Enabling doesn't have to be as obvious as in addiction. It can be much less obvious. An irresponsible person can put upon another to bail them out, out of financial or other problems.

The general rule is "do not do for others what they can do for themselves".

Co-dependents will often drink with a drinker when they would prefer not to drink. Co-dependents will even take part in bank robberies, when they would prefer not to, just because they can't say no! You may think that that is a ridiculous exaggeration – but it is not. I met someone in rehab once, with exactly that history.

Explaining / Making Excuses

An A to Z of Co-Dependence

Sometimes it is necessary to explain yourself to someone, or make an excuse if things haven't gone according to plan. All too often however we co-dependents feel the need to explain ourselves when it is completely unnecessary. It is almost always due to childhood programming. The inner child is trying to deflect potential parental anger.

Instead of saying: "Sorry I'm late, but... excuse excuse...... ". Just say: "Sorry I'm late". Making an excuse actually devalues the apology. The same as when making amends; saying; "I realise that taking your boyfriend and marrying him must have hurt you terribly..." is seriously reduced in value by adding "but if you hadn't got drunk at the party..." or: "but he didn't intend to marry you anyway...".

No "ifs or buts". Say what you mean and mean what you say. Don't minimise your apology. Grovel if you have to. Be humble. Take it on the chin.

Fantasising

See Irresponsibility and addiction.

I retreated into fantasy for most of my life - that is the first 50 years. This had many detrimental results. I didn't bother with my education, career or relationships. And what else is there? Well I didn't overeat or take drugs or fall into any *other* addictions. I was lucky. I was a bit of a love addict I suppose, getting married 3 times.

I came out of it relatively unscathed. This was because of the fantasising. I had never really engaged with reality. This is another example of emotional unavailability. So how did I get out? Well, I put it down to finding myself in a position where I needed to focus hard on other people's problems. I thus had to put myself onto one side and develop some empathy for others. It took quite a few years, and after that I still had to learn to let go of most of the dysfunctional behaviours listed here, in this A-Z.

I see my fantasising as an addiction. It had a real hold over me. These days I find that it doesn't work as a comfort blanket any more. And I thank God (and my Higher Power) for that.

Feelings

A good co-dependent doesn't have feelings - not his own anyway. We take on the feelings of others. What we think they are feeling anyway. Our empathy is a pseudo empathy. We project our own neuroses onto others and feel by proxy. It's much safer. We can shut the difficult feelings off more easily.

If we accidently feel a feeling coming on we can quickly push it down again with a diversionary tactic, such as having a piece of chocolate or phoning a friend to talk about "their stuff". Our ability to deny our feelings is enormous. This way we avoid having to deal with our (painful) issues. We can bury them away for a whole life-time. Our memories can be literally erased. This does not mean they are gone completely. Far from it. The damage done to the psyche remains, and will come out eventually in the form of compulsions, neuroses, addictions, and physical bodily damage. Cancer is strongly linked to un-dealt-with emotional traumas.

If we see others in emotional pain we rush in to fix their feelings. That is, to nullify them, to stop them feeling their feelings. We know how painful it is for us, so we "assume" that they want to get rid of them too.

This is however, not a productive way to deal with painful feelings. We must let them happen. Sit quietly and welcome them. Let the tears fall if necessary. Think about what has triggered the feelings, where does it hurt? Are you hurting more than the immediately obvious cause warrants? Maybe this event has triggered an older wound - from childhood perhaps? What **_was_** that? What was **_your_** part in that? Are you blaming yourself when an adult was really to blame? Was your young self really at fault? Or is that what you were told? You cannot really hold yourself responsible for what happened to you as a child. It will take time (and maybe therapy) to undo this malignant programming.

Fixing Feelings

See also: Feelings

What happens if you begin to feel a (good or bad) feeling?

Do you reach for the wine bottle, bar of chocolate, put the TV on, or begin to fantasise perhaps? This is called "fixing your feelings".

If a feeling comes up - push it down again quickly, deny it. Distract yourself immediately - rescue somebody! Make yourself feel *good*, don't risk feeling *bad* by feeling a bad feeling! It might not be nice!

If we are to grow up at all we must acknowledge our own feelings, and be aware of them continuously. So sit down calmly and re-sist all temptation to distract yourself. Try and get that fleeting feeling back. Where did it come from? What is it saying? Did you do something childish? Did you react badly? Were you unable to join in a conversation with peers?

All the above are quite normal for co-dependents, but a little attention to what is going on will point you in the right direction of making changes.

The 1st step is to resist the temptation to react. Allow yourself to feel the feeling. Next, analyse its source. What co-dependent behaviours were going on? Perhaps you were in fear of authority figures or in child mode with someone that you felt was a surrogate parent to you in some way? Try and imagine the situation again where you behave differently, in a more adult way.

Whatever the behaviour try and imagine it happening in a different way, with you not ex-hibiting any co-dependent behaviours, and not reacting but responding in an adult way.

Generational Dys-functionality

It does appear that a family group will perpetu-ate dysfunctional behaviours through the gen-erations - and that in each succeeding genera-tion the problem becomes more acute. Dys-functional behaviours do not appear to dissi-pate in a family group of their own accord over time. If they did dissipate over time, logically we would not be observing the level of dysfunc-tionality that we are.

I believe that individual behaviours are promul-gated by a set of core beliefs in the family sys-tem, that reinforce the behaviours with each generation. These beliefs are not challenged - they are held to be self-evidently true. (proba-bly no one is even aware of these "rules") From my observations these beliefs lead to serious mental and physical health problems, so much so that the family will cease to function and become a genetic dead-end.

An A to Z of Co-Dependence

I grew up believing that to be a good person one had to:

1. Help / Rescue/ Care-take people
2. Be nice to people
3. Agree with others
4. Be unselfish
5. Not to ask for anything for myself
6. Not to ask questions
7. Pretend nothing is wrong

These behaviours were rewarded with parental attention and praise. Other behaviours were rewarded by being ridiculed, shamed or ignored. Thus I learned that love was conditional, also that I could not rely on adults for support.

I also learned that self-care was a selfish act, getting self-esteem from anything I did for myself was next to impossible, thus self-esteem was always obtained from others, thus I became dependent on others for my sense of wellbeing, and my sense of identity. Without a true sense of independent identity, having safe personal boundaries was next to impossible, thus diminishing any growth in self-esteem that may accidentally occur.

Thus I became trapped in a cycle of dependency. The core beliefs above now needed to be questioned, and relegated to 2nd place behind beliefs about looking after myself and thinking about my own needs, eventually establishing an identity of my own. Thus being able to begin the work of growing up.

Additionally the wider social grouping has societal values that must be adhered to. These can include:

1. Don't complain
2. Don't make a fuss
3. Don't question authority
4. Do what everybody else does

In other words, don't be honest, and don't be yourself. Be what you think other people expect you to be. All these behaviours contribute to staying as a child. Turning away from responsibility for oneself, and adulthood.

Gossiping

I didn't realise how untrustworthy this made me. Just because I didn't have any boundaries doesn't mean that other people don't have boundaries. Learn to respect other people – their boundaries, their possessions, their confidences. Before you share any information, think: Is this any of my business? Would that person rather I didn't share this information? If it really is nothing to do with you, don't say it!

If you have nothing to say about yourself, then ask the other person about themselves. I know some people are very private, and don't share much about themselves, but most people are happy to talk.

Wearing your heart on your sleeve, and telling everybody everything about you is very childish. It's what little children do with mummy and daddy. Step back from that and begin to undo the habit. Act more grown up. Let that become a habit. And you will be more grown up. I believe it is these childhood habits that keep us in child.

Grandiosity

See also Narcissism.

This is perhaps not really a co-dependent characteristic. It is a personality disorder that can affect almost anyone. I think that it is perhaps a response to feelings of insecurity? It appears to counteract feelings of being "less than" others. Or perhaps it is feeling entitled to have the best of everything - but at the expense of others.

Whatever it is, it is a very interesting behavioural trait - intellectually interesting that is. It can be very distressing for those affected by the sufferer.

Typically a person suffering from grandiosity will have no discernible empathy for others (is there any other kind of empathy?) They will talk about themselves incessantly. They will talk

over other people and if they do ever allow anyone else to speak they will immediately steer
the conversation back to themselves and not
remember a thing that anyone else said - usually asking the same questions on meeting the
same person again. If travelling they may well
go first class, even if broke and out of work.
They will only stay in the nicest of hotels - and
demand the lowest rates of course!

It seems to me that a person suffering from low
self-esteem will often have grandiose fantasies
about themselves - as a defence mechanism.

This grandiosity may not be visible to others
and will probably dissipate quickly once a person's self-esteem is raised through adherence
to some therapeutic program.

Grief

Grief appears to be a natural human response
to emotional losses, probably even financial
losses. One could argue that the person was

probably emotionally attached to their wealth. After all one does not get wealthy without putting in some emotional effort into obtaining it.

However, I have known people still apparently suffering from grief, decades after the loss of a loved one. And no amount of therapy seems to shift them from this rut.

I can only conclude that it is some kind of penance for the guilt they feel around the loss. But see Guilt

Guilt

Guilt and shame seem to go hand in hand. If you are suffering unduly or irrationally, from guilt – do seek help. See section on Shame.

Help – Not Asking for it

An A to Z of Co-Dependence

Why don't we ask for help?
Why <u>can't</u> we ask for help?

This, for me, is probably a learned behaviour. At school if I didn't know something I would be humiliated by the teacher if I didn't have all the answers – and asking for help is admitting that I don't know something.

I now have a lifelong irrational dislike (hatred) of teachers and schools. It didn't help that I didn't listen much at school - I kept drifting off into a fantasy world. But see section on Fanta-sising.

How do we rectify this? Practice. It gets pro-gressively easier, as you learn that the world doesn't come to an end when you ask a ques-tion. The ground doesn't open up and swallow you (really).

Find a friend who understands - maybe your sponsor, or someone in Coda. Practice asking a question. Such as "can you help me carry this bag?", moving on to more esoteric things such as "I don't understand boundaries/caretaking/rescuing et cetera, can you help me understand?" Be humble enough to listen, really listen. Then ask questions! See section on asking questions.

Helping Others

We are social animals. We survive as a group, not as individuals. We survive better by pulling together. However there will always be some individuals who take advantage of the group, and act selfishly. Richard Dawkins has a great discussion on this in "The Selfish Gene" (1976). He says that any group (of any species) can only tolerate a limited number of selfish members of the "herd" (before the herd becomes non-viable). That is where we need to set boundaries and step back from our altruism when confronted by selfish behaviour.

We get to feel good about ourselves by helping the group. The group should feedback its appreciation of our efforts and we become more highly valued members of the group (I am referring to humans now - maybe other primates do this to some extent, I don't know). When we are taken advantage of we feel humiliated and bad about ourselves - unless we are co-dependent and have learned to minimise any such feelings (usually as a childhood protection mechanism I would say). Thus co-dependents often allow themselves to be used and abused, not having the appropriate boundaries in place, thus not recognising when it is happening.

Hormones Rule - OK

Massive amounts of various hormones are released into the blood stream when we commence a potentially sexual encounter - particularly for the first time. If that other person really "presses our buttons" then we don't have much of a chance of resisting this insidious turn of events.

An A to Z of Co-Dependence

This extremely addictive "high" is what nature has given us in order to ensure procreation. Without this many people would never enter a sexual relationship, let alone get over their embarrassment about getting naked, and actually have sex. After all, it is a highly irrational thing to do, isn't it Spock?

Unfortunately the accepted wisdom is that this is all there is! This is reinforced by the words of most "pop" songs. Learn to feel nausea at their little trite lies. Movies also must necessarily tell their story in ninety minutes or less, giving further lie to the nature of relationships, by only ever telling part one of a multi part tale.
So everyone gets disappointed when the initial euphoria fades. And moves on, to pastures new.

Another downside is love-addiction. Again Nature has tried to ensure that a couple with a baby stay together, to ensure survival of the progeny. This can lead to new mothers becoming seemingly addicted to the most unsuitable men. Sometimes it seems that the more uncouth, violent and ill-suited they are to be fa-

thers and providers, the more addicted the women become. This is only logical though, isn't it Spock?
Cure for love addiction? Break all contact. Seek help. Urgently.

There is a lot to be said for the "old fashioned" way of doing things. Young people were chaperoned (accompanied on dates). Thus they were prevented from getting into trouble (most of the time). Potential spouses were hand-picked by parents or other relatives from suitable families.

There were still illegitimate babies of course. To understand the intense social pressure against having children outside marriage you must remember two things. One, no welfare state. parish support was minimal. Two, women could not earn a living wage. Also, most people could only just about support themselves - and families were larger, and the risk of disease was high - and no effective antibiotics were available. I know that's more than two, but perm any two from five...

An A to Z of Co-Dependence

The ramifications were enormous. A daughter at home with a new child and no father, was an intolerable burden - everyone would suffer seriously - and she would probably never marry. A lot of people never could afford to marry anyway, but at least they could work. A woman really needed to marry, and marry as well as she could. Ordinary people could not afford to divorce legally. Thus a woman who found herself hitched to a ne'er do well drunkard or whatever, may well leave him and remarry bigamously in another town. She had few other options. Many women were forced by the system (of male domination) into a life of drudgery and/or prostitution. Death was an early and welcome release I would think. This is one of the "old fashioned" ways that I am not advocating!

Today the State tries to take responsibility for everything - and this is not a healthy situation either. For a start it leads to dependency. Secondly the State has not got infinite resources. And dependency seems to breed dependency! Thirdly, when the time comes for the state to withdraw support it finds that it gets voted out

of office and cannot do what it needs to do.
Thus Democracy itself may succumb under the
weight of the welfare burden.

Identity - having one

If one has been seriously co-dependent for any
length of time, one will have lost a lot of one's
sense of identity. I certainly did. How can we
rebuild it? Where do we start?

Read the section on Boundaries. If your boundaries are weak, then I believe your sense of
identity is necessarily weak. Do you know what
you want - for you? To "help others" is just not
good enough. Do you really "love" yourself?

Are you doing the work you wanted to do? Or
are you just earning a crust, and getting drunk
on a Friday night? Do you buy yourself what
you really want - that shiny MX5 - or settle for
that rusty old Fiesta? (I waited 37 years to buy

myself that sailing dinghy I wanted - almost too late!) Is your wardrobe plain and drab and semi worn out - or does it reflect the joie de vivre - that you will be feeling soon?

What do you want? Think about it. Make a list. If you don't know what you want you won't know when the Universe (God, Life, whatever) gives it to you! (NB If you find it hard to make a list of what you want from life then you are seriously ill with Codependence). Just make a list of what somebody else might want – if you can't get started.

All these things need to be attacked simultaneously, to begin defining yourself. As you spring into existence, you will need to protect this fledgling person with some serious boundaries.

Start here. A person whose self-worth is obtained from others or from possessions is at the mercy of those persons or things. I believe self-worth gives rise to self-regard and ultimately to self itself. One's identity is one's definition of self. Thus when there is no boundary between oneself and others then one's definition of self, i.e. identity, becomes blurred and fragile (i.e. malleable). Usually identity fails to develop in the first place, at puberty. Thus having self-worth, independent of others is vital to future well- being, as is having clear boundaries between you and others.

It is not simply a case of defining boundaries. In itself this is hard enough for co-dependents to do. One must develop independent self-regard, giving rise to a stronger sense of identity. Only then is the self able to put the boundaries in place and feel confident enough to enforce them.

Examples of boundaries:

1. Do not call me after 10pm. This should be made clear in advance.
2. Do not ask to borrow my car/money etc. Be ready with a response such as: "I'm sorry, I realise that you need help right now, but I do not lend my car to anyone, to avoid any mishaps."

An A to Z of Co-Dependence

Decide on your personal rules and try to stick to them. Identify where you have been put upon, and felt resentful. Consider making a boundary around it. This is hardest to do with one's own children.

Why would anyone become so dependent? Self-worth can fail to develop during childhood due to parental behaviours. These can be all or some of the following:

1. Abandonment
2. Criticism
3. Over control
4. Mixed messages
5. Ridicule
6. Any kind of abuse
7. Lack of support
8. Addictions (including addictive behaviours)
9. Parental mental illness

And there are probably many more.

Regaining Self-Worth. A tricky one. This will take time and a bit of effort on your part. Hopefully it will be fun. Being willing to change is main requirement. You will need help. Go to a self-help group such as Coda. Work the steps.

1. Identify the incidents that damaged you. These are the events that still rankle 40 or 50 years later
2. Share these with your sponsor (Coda terminology for Mentor)
3. Start rebuilding yourself. You are your own parent now.
4. Identify what you are afraid of - what is stopping you?
5. Go to meetings - find out what has worked for others
6. Identify what dreams you never followed through

What dreams did you have as a teenager?

1. Tour Europe by bicycle
2. Climb Kilimanjaro
3. Learn to sail/ski/play guitar
4. Live by the sea
5. Sing in a band

Decide to do one of them soon. Make a new list of the dreams you have now...

Your lack of self-worth has meant that you never achieved any of you dreams. There are many tricks, such as looking at yourself in the mirror and saying: "You're a great person!" and mean it. Practice saying "No" as well, to some imaginary person sitting opposite you. If you are facing a difficult conversation with someone, run through possible scenarios in your head. Have something ready to say for as many situations as you can imagine. Your responses may surprise you.

Irresponsibility

Acting without thinking: impulsivity. Stems from unwillingness to make the effort to think things through. Magical thinking. Everything will come right in the end, I don't have to think about it.

An A to Z of Co-Dependence

When the situation becomes serious, such as problem with debts, the person may become embroiled in denial. Problems seem so big that they cannot see that a solution is even remotely possible, so they blot out the situation with more spending. There is a temporary feel-good factor, thus the cycle continues. There is usually a negative attitude towards asking for help. Thus the bailiffs are usually on the doorstep when the person arrives at the citizens' advice bureau or wherever.

Note: The CAB are *not* miracle workers. They often need three weeks' notice before you get an appointment. ..

If this is *you* then realise that the sooner you get help the easier it will be to get out of your predicament. The longer you wait the harder you're making things for yourself.

Drink and drugs and having crazy people around you will all contribute to the madness. Things are going to change whether you like it or not. Do you want to have some say in the matter or not? It's up to you.

It's not all about You

In this illness we can easily become obsessed about others.

- What are they thinking about me?
- Why are they unkind to me?
- Why don't they talk to me?

In reality probably nothing is going on, they are just going about their business. They have their own stuff. You're not on their radar. It's not about you at all. It never was. Except in your head.

Recognize that other people are not there just to feed your ego (because your ego is dependent on them). You are just another person (whatever you may think). If you want normal relationships with normal people you will have to meet them half way. You have to take notice of them, feed their egos now and again. You have to talk to them, listen to what they say and really take an interest. Ask questions. You can't fake genuine caring. (Oxymoron)

Judging / Being Judgmental

When we feel badly about ourselves, we tend to look at others judgmentally, saying to ourselves that they are "not as good as us", "not on the program", "not as intelligent", not this or not that. This gives us the illusion of some self-esteem. Our attitude eventually gets noticed, and we are regarded as "weirdoes". Thus we achieve less than nothing.

If we can, we should try to treat everyone with respect and love. Politeness costs nothing. We should try to retain an open mind, even if others invite us to be judgmental about a colleague.

Keeping it to You

Finding the right form of words is essential if we are to move into adulthood.

Whenever we use the word "you" we risk being an accuser. This can quickly make others uncooperative and antagonistic.

Saying: "Your car is in the way" for instance, could be better expressed as: "We need to keep the driveway clear for the doctor's car".

Saying: "You always forget my birthday", is accusing and probably not totally true. Try: "I am upset that you forgot my birthday" will be more likely to get the response you really wanted.

Saying: "You don't care about me" will get a bad reaction. Try: "I sometimes feel that you don't care about me very much".

Use "I" statements. I feel that..., I would prefer to..., I believe...

Keep it to yourself. You don't know what other people are thinking. You may think you do, but you don't <u>really</u> know.

Using the work "You" is essentially controlling. Let it go. Does it really matter that much? Just keep yourself safe. Don't accuse, judge or assume...

Letting Go

Let go of false beliefs;

- There's not enough money/food/love
- I'm not good enough
- I must help/advise others
- I must rescue/care-take/people-please
- Others need me to tell them what to do
- That something outside me can "fix" me

Let go of "neediness". If you think someone or something outside of you can fix that "emptiness" inside you, think again. This is classic dependency. You may be dependent on outside things for your self-worth, Identity, values, etc. Whilst you are dependent in this way you will be trapped in immature reactivity. Others *can* manage without you. You *can* manage without them. Think about what <u>you</u> want for <u>you</u>. The world won't end if you leave others to get on with their own lives for a while.

Do you feel at all resentful of others putting on you? Always asking you to do things they could do themselves? Taking advantage of you? Are you sure you are not enabling them? Just let them manage without you for a while. They will respect you more, you will respect yourself more. Let go of focussing on other's needs. Focus on your own. Focussing on others is really avoidance of looking at your own needs. Do you think, deep down, that you are not worth it? If you don't think you're worth it, others certainly won't,

Let go of;

- Telling lies / half-truths / exaggerating

An A to Z of Co-Dependence

- Denial (of your behaviours)
- Guilt / Shame
- Being Judgmental
- Hoarding
- Dependency

Let go of anything you are using as a distraction from looking within;

- Drink / cigarettes / food / drugs
- Socialising obsessively
- Games (particularly electronic)
- Exercise (excessive)
- Obsessing
- Shopping
- Rescuing/ caretaking
- Fantasising
- TV / Internet
- Gambling
- Pornography

Try to see it for what it is - a distraction, that is holding up your recovery, delaying the time when you can feel more joyful, free, clear headed and at peace with yourself.

Letting Go of Outcomes

Just do the footwork and what happens, happens.
Keep it to yourself. That is, don't try and do other people's thinking for them. Just say; I think, I feel, etc.
Think before you do anything.
Just do the foot work – do the next right thing.
Finding your voice, speaking your truth at meetings.
Sit with your feelings, learn to be with yourself.
Avoid distracting behaviours.

Listening

Learn to really listen. Forget about what <u>you</u> have to say.

Co-dependents think they are good listeners, perhaps they are, but are they good hearers? That is, do they really <u>hear</u> what is being said? I think not, in many cases.

When you can ask meaningful questions during the conversation, and not be trying all the time to bring the conversation around to you, then perhaps you *are* really <u>hearing</u> the other person.

Step twelve, carrying the message, somewhat perversely, can be looked on as simply being there and "hearing".

Love Is - Not what you think

When two people realise that they are interested in each other something strange often happens. That something is a massive shot of powerful love hormones into their blood streams. This is a very pleasant experience that enables the protagonists to overcome their shyness, or normal caution and move on to the next stage. As far as nature is concerned this next stage is procreation and staying together to successfully bring the child to the point of repeating the (ridiculous) exercise.

This initial chemically induced love is short lived however. It is not "real" love, as the Greeks would have it (they had about six words for love I believe). If you regularly rapidly fall out of love and go looking for someone else, then you probably have erroneous ideas about love. You may even be a "love addict".

Most people seem to have the romantic idea that there is that "special someone" out there, who will fulfil all their desires/needs/fantasies – and make them "whole". There may be that person, but will it last? This myth is propagated and perpetuated by popular songs. Learn to feel nausea at the words of love songs, particularly those of the '50s and early '60s.

Co-dependents are "needy" people. That is, they need love, usually that of the parent who

95

was emotionally or physically unavailable during their formative years. Needy people feel that they will be made whole by this other. It is true that they are only half a person. However they will almost always attract another needy person.

Thus two people get together, each thinking that the other will meet their needs, and are blissfully unaware that the other has such huge expectations of them. Neither has a clue of how to "give" in a relationship. Does this sound like a recipe for a successful long-term relationship? A disastrous one perhaps. An emotionally healthy individual who gets pulled in by a co-dependent will soon extricate themselves.

Whatever you do, don't have children, get a mortgage or go into business with a co-dependent (even if you are co-dependent too), unless you insist on learning the hard way (like me). Actually, people generally seem to prefer learning the hard way.

Alcoholics, addicts etc. are almost always co-dependents - or worse (see Sociopath etc.). Not all co-dependents are addicted to substances however. They may be fantasists, children of addicts, love or sex addicts, amongst many others. (they can also be very charming I might add). Essentially co-dependents are addicted to (dependent upon) other people.

So how do you "do" relationships? Work at it. Is this person worth your time and effort? If so, put the effort in, or move on to someone who is. Don't be mean with money, your time or your compliments, but be sincere. Get to know this person. Do you have values and interests that are compatible? Listen to what they have to say. (really listen - and ask questions to show you're listening). How functional are they? Do they perpetually go on about their mother, resort to alcohol, complain about things but ignore your suggestions? Extricate yourself. They're not your problem. Do you behave like that? Get help.

If their parents / siblings have good relationships and functional behaviours then there is a good chance they will too. However the opposite is also true. Keep away from drinkers, smokers, drug takers, even multiple divorcees and long term unemployed are probably losing bets.

Other dysfunctional traits are living in squalor, not washing enough, not eating properly, not paying bills, being chronically and unnecessarily in debt, hoarding, general unmanageability. You get the picture. Be hard-nosed about finding a life partner!

Minimising

- Harm caused to self
- harm caused to others
- refusal to accept severity of issues/potential for harm/damage/loss
- inability to accept urgency of the situation/need for action
- denial of responsibility
- inability to face the damaging repercussions of actions such as excessive drinking, eating, drug-taking
- partner's problems / feelings

Mirroring Other's Feelings

A good co-dependent, not being aware of his own feelings, will look at others around him and attempt to mirror their feelings. He will thus live vicariously through the lives of others. He will not really know of course, what others are really feeling. His reality will thus be entirely imaginary. In this imaginary world there are no bad feelings and reality rarely disturbs him.

Mirroring Others

Curiously, when we perceive co-dependent or other dysfunctional behaviours in others, we often find it in ourselves if we look closely enough. Some mysterious force brings it to our attention this way, by showing it to us in others. The mystery deepens!

Narcissism

This is not really a co-dependent behaviour itself but when identified in others we can perhaps approach them with greater love and understanding. If we know what to expect we can take it less personally, when the narcissist's behaviour eventually makes us resentful.

We can step back and not be co-dependent around them. Maintaining strong boundaries around the narcissist is vital!

Narcissistic character traits
- Only the narcissist exists. Even their children are just extensions of themselves.
- The narcissist needs constant affirmation that they are "loved" or they get severe abandonment issues-unlike psychopaths and sociopaths.

- Narcissists don't really hear what any-one says to them unless it is what they want to hear
- They don't care about anyone else - because they don't exist
- Other people are only useful in order to bolster the narcissist's ego
- The Narcissist talks incessantly
- The Narcissist talks over people

Very likely narcissism exists on a scale from barely narcissistic to totally narcissistic. Perhaps most of us are somewhere on the scale at some point in our lives? Perhaps young children could be said to be narcissists - before they reach the age of 8 or 9, when they begin to become more aware of other people. Perhaps it is the case that the adult narcissist has failed to develop normally?

See also grandiosity, Psychopath and Sociopath

Needing to be

Needed

1. Those of us who get our sense of identity from others are often/normally said to be "dependent".

2. This usually arises from the circumstances of our upbringing.

3. If our parent's love was perceived as being in any way conditional, then a s a child we will learn behaviours that will enable us to "earn" this love (it could be said that this type of love is not "real" love).

4. We then may have become "helpful" or highly obedient - whatever it took.

5. We would then tend to be constantly monitoring our care-givers, looking for opportunities to "perform" and get our reward.

6. We have thus learned that love and affection are obtained outside ourselves - and we may become so obsessed with this process that we are constantly on the lookout for someone (anyone) who needs us.

7. Thus we have developed a need to be needed - a "needy" personality. If we find a similar person, who is also a potential partner, we think we have just found our "soul mate". Thus we pair up and form a co-dependent partnership.

8. Unfortunately this is not likely to be a healthy relationship - both parties are seeking to receive unconditional love, but neither know How to give it (or are even aware of what they or their partner wants)

What does Conditional Love look like?

1. If mummy says to her child something as innocuous as "If you tidy your room, you can have a sweetie", the child learns something about bribery. It is more serious when a mother withholds her affection over some issue. I believe it is even more serious when a mother gives more attention to say, a TV program. The conflicting messages received will likely seriously confuse the child.

2. Depending on the age of the child and the seriousness of the issue the parent must be careful to establish firm rules (boundaries) but not make his/her love conditional in any way.

3. It must be appreciated that before the age of about 12 the child's frontal lobes - and hence any significant moral reasoning ability will not have developed. Clear and firm rules are needed. Expecting the child to process complex issues is not on. The child will need to be able to understand that the rules are fair and consistent however.

4. If the child comes to believe that love is conditional, they will come to understand that they are not inherently worthwhile and will seek self-worth through other people, or things (money, possessions etc.).

5. The resulting damage may never be rectified and lead to an unfulfilled life, divorce(s) and alcoholism - or worse.

Negativity

Why do so many of us (me included) seem to cling to our negativity? What's in it for us?

Primarily I think that it is a way of avoiding personal responsibility - for our recovery. Whilst we can blame other people for our problems we can avoid accepting our part in it. So by focussing on the negative we can continue to justify our inaction. We may get a bit of attention from our self-pity stance, but we must realise that it is our inner child at work. Take your inner child to one side and tell him to lay off the self-pity - it's pathetic.

As always it is the avoiding that is the reward for our dysfunctional behaviour. We don't have to face the truth. We are pathologically afraid of the truth. Deep down we fear that we are really to blame. In fact the truth will always set us free, emotionally, psychologically and spiritually. The truth may imprison you physically, but it's probably better to do 5 years in the nick, than spend the next 40 years or so in an emotional prison (and probably end up with physical ailments).

Keep a journal of your negative thoughts. Now make a list of the positive things that have happened in your life, now think about this week. Keep focussing on the positive. You will find there are plenty of good things happening around you. What are you being negative about? Is it really such a big issue for you if there are floods in Australia? Get on with <u>your</u> life.

Now, be realistic. What are your worst fears? What have you <u>really</u> got to lose?

Essentially you have a life. You are unique. If you don't live your life to the full, if you don't feel any of the joy that is rightfully yours, then YOU are the loser. Nobody else will really care. How can they? Nobody really cares about anybody else that much, and certainly they shouldn't care more about others than they care about themselves. So start caring about yourself -because nobody else will if you don't.

Identify your sources of fear, look at them realistically with your sponsor or counsellor, and create an action plan to negate them one by one. Keep checking your progress and revise as necessary.

No - Inability to Say

What part of the word "No" don't you understand? I hear this regularly from my partner.

Are you able to say "No"? That is, not for trivial things. Maybe someone wants you to help them in some way? Do you think before you answer? Or do you always say "yes" immediately? (And later feel resentful?)

Can you say "no" to that extra drink, when you have really had enough?

An A to Z of Co-Dependence

Does it actually hurt to say "No"? Are you secretly afraid that they won't like you anymore? Is your friendship really that shallow?

Do these "friends" only call you when they want something? Do you really need friends like these?

If you do have this problem you will need to break the habit of always saying "Yes". Have some handy phrases ready such as "I will need to check my diary first, and come back to you". Or "I think I have something else on that day, can I come back to you?"

In time you will find it easier to think on your feet and, not feeling rushed you will remember whether you are free or not and you will feel sufficiently secure in yourself to make a decision that you can keep to, and not feel resentful about.

Parent Adult Child Ego States

Read "Counselling for Toads" (Robert de Board) before you go any further. It's a great read. Very wise. Unbelievably moving (for me). I didn't realise it was my story until I read it for the second time.

Basically, you won't get much out of reading this unless you are in Adult.

Parent Surrogates

It is tempting for a co-dependent, when interacting with more functional people, to react to them as parent substitutes. The co-dependent will obviously be in child mode at this point. This is not a good place to be for an adult, so be that adult.

An A to Z of Co-Dependence

Remember to pause before reacting and make considered responses. You must break that old programming! Recognise when you are with people who you look up to, and possibly admire. Remember that they are not your mummy or daddy!

Passive Aggressive Behaviour

Essentially this is controlling behaviour. This must be how codependents go about controlling others. By non-cooperation, by not speaking, by sulking. I didn't think that I was at all controlling until I was introduced to the idea of passive-aggressive behaviour. Doh!

People Pleasing

This is just what it says on the tin.

In order to get their needs met, the co-dependent tries to manipulate people into loving them and needing them, maybe even making them dependent on the codependent.

The problem is that the downside (for everybody) can be enormous, and it gets bigger and

111

bigger as the co-dependent tries harder and harder to get their needs met.

As a result the co-dependent can:
- tell lies
- over-commit themselves
- be unable to say no
- neglect their own needs
- Be unaware of their own feelings
- become resentful if taken advantage of
- let others down
- damage the very relationships they are trying to protect
- be unable to transition to adulthood

The victim May:
- become resentful
- Begin to dislike the co-dependent
- take advantage of the co-dependent
- make fun of the co-dependent
- distance themselves from the codepend-ent.

The big problem was that I thought "people pleasing" was the way to solve the problem that I thought I had. In fact I was making the problem much worse.

I felt the same about rescuing and caretaking. The more I indulged in those behaviours the worse my codependence became. The result was that I was unable to behave as an adult. I was stuck in child.

Power - Taking it from someone

Don't give your Power away to someone else.

There is an old (12-step) adage: "don't do for someone what they can do for themselves"

Because if you do, you end up making decisions for them, and they really lose the power to make those decisions.

- You may make the wrong decision and cause real problems

113

- you may well make the other person resentful
- you may well become resentful yourself
- you fail to attend to your own problems

If you are asked to help someone with something, try and involve that person with the process as much as possible.

Don't do anything you have not been expressly asked to do. Don't make assumptions (see assuming).

You really don't know what is best for others, you only imagine you do!

Procrastinating

I have just restarted work on this A-Z after a four-year hiatus! The list of topics had just got larger and larger. I got disheartened. I needed more recovery. I always had a good excuse. Today I have covered 9 topics already-and I'll do another 9 before teatime! Tomorrow the job will be done, well the 1st draft anyway. I'll put it out there for comment and correction. I know I have made a lot of grand assertions and generalisations that not everyone will agree with. But it's important that this work is not misleading in any way. That's probably all I need to say about procrastination.

Projecting

If a co-dependent feels angry (for example) he or she may accuse their spouse/parents et cetera of being angry, when they are not. Thus the co-dependent has projected their feelings onto another.

The projectee may then become angry themselves. Perhaps this then facilitates recognition of the feelings in the co-dependent, who was unable to recognise his/her feelings. Thus the co-dependent can then express anger in return.

Projection of emotions is not restricted to anger.

Psycho-path/Sociopath

See also Narcissist.

These are not specifically co-dependent behaviours. Just learn to recognise them and keep well away! If forced into their company - maintain strong boundaries!

Both types care only about themselves. They believe that they are right about everything, and have to be in control of everyone and everything.

The wisdom of the Internet sees psychopaths as cold and calculating, whereas sociopaths are more reactive and impulsive. Both types will blame anyone and everyone else for their failures and make up the most fatuous of excuses and expect them to be believed.

Sociopaths will generally form very weak relationships with others, whereas psychopaths may appear to form strong relationships but they will invariably be faking it.

Examples Hitler, Stalin, Napoleon, Donald Trump et cetera. It would appear that political power attracts these 2 groups of people. Perhaps anyone who wants power should be barred standing for office?

Questions – Not asking them

In many families asking questions is simply not allowed. There are probably family secrets to be kept. Maybe a relative is alcoholic or someone is divorced. These things were so shameful at one time that they were forbidden topics. So not understanding what subjects were, and were not allowed, the child learns not to ask any questions at all, in order to be safe.

How do we fix this? Again practice, practice, practice. When listening to someone relate a story, really listen. Take a real interest. If you hear something that needs more explanation then try and ask a question. "I didn't understand that last point - can you explain?" Or "who is this person you are referring to?" And "why did that happen?" Again it gets easier the more you do it. But you must really, _really_ listen and take a real interest in the tale.

Reacting versus Responding

A good co-dependent will react without thinking much of the time. Thus old behaviours are repeated ad nauseam and reinforced continuously. And may never be never questioned.

In Coda we learn to take a deep breath, think twice before acting - hopefully in a more considered way. We use compassion and understanding in our response in any situation. Thus the old reactive patterns of behaviour are progressively weakened, and new, more adult and more functional behaviours take their place.

Rescuing / Fixing Others

I learned as a child that to get my parents approval I had to be a "good" boy. This meant being helpful to them - and by extension, when I was older, that to be a good person I had to be "helpful" to all parental figures. I had learned to get my self-esteem from others. I was now dependent on others and used inordinate amounts of time and mental effort to find ways of rescuing, caretaking and people-pleasing other people, instead of looking at myself, and finding that self-esteem within.

This, taken to an extreme (as I did) can lead to:

An A to Z of Co-Dependence

1. Offering advice, when not actually asked to do so - potentially annoying and leading to "persecutor, rescuer, victim" scenarios. (drama triangle)
2. Being unable to say "No" to any request. This can lead to becoming a "doormat" with consequent loss of self-esteem. (and actually saying "No" lead to such feelings of guilt..)
3. Rescuing - offering to help - anyone, with anything. This sometimes led me to becoming overcommitted, no time for myself or partners or children, who should have been my real concerns.
4. The inability to say "No" inevitably means that Co-dependents are not Trustworthy! Something they would be profoundly unable to believe, but consider it like this: A co-dependent unable to say "No" will react (positively,being unable to be negative) to anyone in front of them. They will find it extremely hard to remember their commitments to others not actually present! Thus often get themselves into a real co-dependent muddle.

5. Caretaking others - exactly as it says, but to the exclusion of oneself - a co-dependent will not look after himself, wash, wear nice clothes, be aware of what he likes, wants or needs. All power is handed over to the "other".

6. The co-dependent will become hyper-vigilant to the perceived needs of others (see Assuming/making assumptions!), ready to jump in and rescue. His/her own needs are neglected totally.

The above scenarios have got me into so much trouble. It has only been by having had it pointed out to me (in a kindly way) that by putting other people before my partner I was not putting her first (obvious when you put it like that). And if I wanted a relationship with her I had better start putting her first!

I had to learn to stop and think about what I was doing. I had to stop REACTING and start RESPONDING. This involves thought! I had to learn to stop and think.

Then to say "I'll have to check my diary" or whatever. Later I could remember other commitments I had, and actually say "No" immediately. This hurt at first. I still get the urge to rescue, but it is getting easier.

So what is the "pay off"? What do I get out of it? (Rescuing)

7. I feel good about myself - I am worth something to somebody (was I not valued as a child?)
8. I have temporarily "fixed" my feelings of low self-worth (being a low value door-mat)
9. Somebody thinks I am a "good" person. (I will be supported)
10. Maybe somebody will help me should I need it?

All these things come from Child. I was treating the person I was rescuing as a Parent. I wanted the approval of a parental figure to fix my feelings (low self-esteem etc.).

An A to Z of Co-Dependence

Fixing Others.

> If a rescuer sees someone hurting, the impulse to "rescue" is enormous. What we are really seeking to do is to nullify the bad feelings the other person has. This is probably because we are empathising and feeling those feelings too, and we don't want them! So we try to "fix" that person. (See Taking on Other's feelings)
>
> We can do this by:
>
> 11. Handing over a box of tissues in a meeting
> 12. Telling them that "worse things happen at sea"
> 13. Talking about something else
> 14. Offering a cup of tea, or whatever

All of these things effectively deny that person the validity of their feelings. If we really want to help, perhaps all we should do is be there and listen.

I have learned to think of rescuing as interfering. I no longer interfere in other people's lives. I no longer try to fix their feelings.

I ask myself "Is this any of my business? Is this my problem?" If not, and it usually is not, I keep my mouth shut!

There are people of course, who try to make their problems into your problems. Be polite and empathise. Listen, and give them the benefit of the doubt and offer help and advice if this is what they want. If it becomes obvious that they are not going to do anything apart from continue to use you, then keep your distance!

Relationships

Parents

My relationship with my parents stayed as a "child to parent" relationship until it was pointed out to me that I was still reacting as a child towards them. Having got some recovery I was able to change my behaviour and my relationship with my parents changed very much for the better. See reacting versus responding.

Higher Power

While still behaving very much as a child I think I was still quite narcissistic. I was certainly passive-aggressive controlling and selfish, whilst believing I was completely the opposite of course. Whilst in child mode I could hardly make any sense of having a relationship with a higher power. With a transition to a more adult outlook I have a better relationship with a higher power.

Authority Figures

A hangover from schooldays is that I was greatly in fear of authority figures. I simply didn't know how to deal with them. I always anticipated a negative outcome of any interaction. Again it has taken transition to adulthood and practice to leave this fear behind and I now find dealing with any authority figures relatively easy.

Peers

Looking back I can see that I always tried to get love and attention from my friends. I did this by rescuing and caretaking. I was always the one offering to help although I could never ask for it. I was the one giving advice, but never taking it.

I can't imagine how I kept so many friends! (Perhaps they were co-dependent too?) I must have been very irritating, to say the least.

These days I don't give advice, I only help when asked and I accept gifts and money graciously, when offered. I don't lend books, I don't tell people what films to watch and I don't make people watch hundreds and hundreds of slides of my travels, as I have been wont to do in the past!

Special Relationships – i.e. Romantic ones. Do try and remember to keep these special. I.e. – put them first!
I was really bad at this – always trying to help everyone equally – and expecting my "other half" to understand! She did alright – she wasn't number one! And that is what I had to learn – and quickly too.

Relationships with Dysfunctional People

In general dysfunctional people will find themselves in relationships with other dysfunctional people. A reasonably well-functioning individual will quickly tire of the company of someone who is dysfunctional in some way.

Thus a co-dependent will often find themselves married (or in a close relationship) to a control freak, an alcoholic or a person with some other less than desirable personality characteristic(s). Depending on circumstances it may result in a long, but dysfunctional (dependent) relationship. Or it may break up very quickly. Neither outcome should be regarded as acceptable!

It is very often observed, in 12-step meetings, that people with some small measure of recovery will attempt to form relationships with persons they are attracted to at the meeting. This usually ends in tears and does not generally assist in a person's recovery - usually the opposite occurs. This can obviously be quite disastrous in the case of recovery from addiction to substances...

Responsibility (Personal)

To yourself, to others and to the world.

An A to Z of Co-Dependence

Your responsibility to the world may depend a lot on your philosophy of life. So I won't go into that too deeply.

It came to me a couple of years ago that the word I had to focus on was "Responsibility". It was a minor epiphany, a pivotal moment. No trumpets sounded, the Earth didn't move, but something inside me did. It was the next port of call on the journey. I set the auto pilot and went back to sleep....

Now, here I am attempting to get to grips with all this stuff (all _my_ stuff).

The reality is that I have almost entirely ignored the revelation. Not that I don't believe it, but because I don't want to be responsible for myself. There I've said it. Time to explore what it means.

As young children, obviously no one expects us to be responsible. Some children are forced to take care of dysfunctional parents, younger siblings etc.. But that is different from accepting personal responsibility.

An A to Z of Co-Dependence

Growing up should mean accepting more and more responsibility for one self. This does not happen automatically - or overnight. We may have adopted self-protection behaviours in childhood that actually get in the way of growing up - unless we can let go of them.

Becoming aware of these behaviours, and their effect on us and others, is key to letting go of them and starting to grow up.

So what are you responsible for, as an adult?

1. Work. What will you do with your life? How will you prepare for that?
2. Your place in society. How will you contribute to the common weal? (look it up)
3. Your health. What you eat and drink, the amount of exercise you take
4. Having healthy habits - no drugs or excessive drinking
5. Your education. Ignorance is not bliss, nor is it a defence. It's a liability. Are you?

6. Your family. Parents, siblings, wife/husband, children. Mutual interdependency. Can anyone guarantee that the state will *always* be there for you?

7. Your personal growth. There will be no consolation in being old and grey if you are still acting like a teenager.

8. Staying within the law. Getting fined for speeding is irresponsible. Losing your licence for drink/drive offences is grossly irresponsible. Robbing banks is definitely going to get you into big trouble. And the effects on wife and children will be immeasurable.

9. Doing a fair days work. Turn up on time, do your work as best you can, treat the company and its property with respect - and expect the same in return.

10. Treat other people with respect - and expect the same in return.

11. Treat public property with respect, encourage others to do the same.

12. Don't cheat the system. Pay your taxes, don't make false insurance claims.

13. Vote. Engage with the democratic process. It may be less than perfect, but it's

not going to improve if we let the politicians run it, is it?

14. Being honest inside and outside is key to being a viable responsible adult.

This way you know you've nothing to hide, and nothing to be ashamed of.

My score? Don't ask (getting better)

Well, that's you and others, now about the world.

This finite planet is exactly that. Finite. I believe we have a responsibility to consume as little as we really need to. To waste as little as we possible, to recycle, reuse and repair wherever possible. Individually we may not make much difference, but we can set an example. Also, if we can grow up and free ourselves from our prejudices, then there is a faint possibility of a viable future for mankind.

What will be your legacy? Fifteen worn out cars, three dysfunctional children and a battered wife? I hope to leave more than that. I mean less than that.

I hope that this "booklet" will bring hope to at least one person. I also hope I can pass on my skills and enthusiasms to my children - and others. If I am lucky the world will be a better place for my having been here.

What is life about anyway? Is it meaningless, random chance having produced humankind? Or is it meaningful? It cannot be a bit meaning-ful, or largely meaningless. It must be either wholly meaningless or wholly meaningful I would postulate. Logically that is. So, I am go-ing for wholly meaningful, the other being a dead end so to speak.

Thus we are now faced with the ultimate in re-sponsibility. What is our responsibility in a world that has meaning? What does it all mean? What can it mean? What could be the purpose of a meaningful universe? Does our individual physical incarnation have meaning too? I believe that would be a logical conclu-sion. It may mean that our experiences in life are valuable, both collectively and individually. In which case our objective should be to experience life to its fullest. We should not fear life or its experiences, rather fear not living life to the full, and thus not achieving what we are here for. If only we knew what that was!

Right – Being

Giving advice is essentially saying that you know it all. Get humble. Always add the words: "In my view" or "As far as I am aware."., "To the best of my knowledge" etc. If you are guessing or if you don't know, say so.

Role Models

Be aware that you are the role models for your offspring, just as your parents were your role models. If you blame your parents for your behaviours then your children will blame you for

theirs. You owe it to your offspring to get recovery! They may never thank you for it as they
may never know, but your life will be that much
better.

Sabotage - Self

See also: Victimhood

This is a weird one. Sometimes it appears that
we deliberately make stupid decisions, or do
stupid things that make matters worse for us.
Maybe it is to reaffirm our negative view of
ourselves, as we attempt to stay in victimhood,
so we can continue to blame others. Again we
are refusing to accept responsibility for our
lives and our decisions.

Shame

Did you grow up with a deep sense of personal
shame? Most of us did. Exactly why can be hard

and painful to pinpoint. Letting go of it can become easier as we dig into it and understand its causes.

As our recovery progresses we will find that our shame dissipates slowly but surely. Understanding and accepting our shame is an essential part of our recovery and letting it go.

In the beginning it can seem that we are not making any progress - only uncovering more and more painful episodes from our lives - ones that we had done our best to repress and hide (from ourselves) for decades (I do believe that these hurts will come out as physical dis-eases eventually if not addressed - book: Louise Hay; " You can heal your life") but it does seem that it is all necessary groundwork.

This is yet another reason why we should not attempt this inner work alone. We need the encouragement and emotional support of our sponsor (mentor) to keep us on track and point out our progress to us. Otherwise as good co-dependents we would of course minimise our successes. Make good use of your sponsor - it helps him/her as well in their recovery. It's not all about YOU.

How has this feeling of shame arisen?

If a young child is ignored or abused in any way, i.e. told he/she is stupid or bad etc. the child will accept what they are told. Children are programmed to believe in their parents. This is their way to survival normally. It follows therefor that the child must come to believe that it is defective in some way, compared to its parents. Thus he/she becomes ashamed of who they are - and attempts to hide in some way.

The child's core belief is "I am not good enough". He tries to address the situation by "people pleasing" and generally saying and doing what he thinks will be acceptable to others - and not daring to be his genuine self.

Shame will effectively prevent transition to proper adulthood - these childhood protection mechanisms will continue to dominate as long as the shame persists. Shame will derail any potential meaningful relationships making them always either mutually co-dependent or parent-child relationships.

Make a list of negative things that were said to you as a child (you will be able to remember lots of them). Think of parents and teachers particularly, but include everyone. You may have been bullied by older siblings perhaps.

Did you hear things like:
- You'll never be any good at music/art/maths..
- You're stupid/useless/an idiot...
- You're ugly/fat/short...
- We're poor because of you
- What will everyone think of you?

Did you expect help and support but
- You were ignored
- You were told to do it yourself
- No one had time for you
- You were told to "grow-up"

Did your main care-givers give you unconditional love and support? Or did they:
- Devote themselves to their hobbies

138

- Give priority to younger or disabled siblings
- Have addictions (alcohol/cigarettes/porn/work/gambling)
- Become separated /divorced
- Work away from home for long periods
- Drag you around the country from school to school, without telling you or explaining anything, or caring that you had left your friends behind, never to be heard of again?

Did "they" expect you to be an adult, even as a child, then berate you for not being an adult? Did they over react to minor misdemeanours (shout/threaten/bully)? Or treat you with understanding?

Any or all of these things can lead the child to conclude that it is of little or no importance. He /she will attempt to hide, and may well disappear into a fantasy word. If you hear: "Oh, he's a dreamer" said about you , that's not a good sign. I spent fifty years in fantasy land and it didn't achieve anything except a wasted fifty years. Equally the child may disappear into addictions etc.

Some children rebel against being abused in this way. They become destructive - and get negative attention - possibly by running away from home and abandoning the parents! I believe that if too many of the above negative traits are present the child has no option but to believe that it is an inherently bad person, and shame becomes the dominant controlling emotion. The parent then achieves their objective of subduing and controlling the child - at the expense of the child's healthy development.

What now?
Do the work. Write about it. Share it with your sponsor. Re-live it all. Feel the emotions. Realise that it was the inner child that was hurt. The adult in you must tell the inner child that he/she is safe now.

Smokescreens

It can often be noticed in highly dysfunctional people, that they accuse others of the very behaviours they themselves are guilty of! The other person is probably much less guilty than they are, perhaps not even guilty at all. The accuser is unconsciously aware of their own behaviour, and is seeking to put up a "smokescreen" to confuse the other. This deliberate presenting of an untruth as a truth confuses and undermines a co-dependent particularly, as they are highly susceptible to suggestion.

Sub-texts

Be very careful of what you say and to whom. You may be giving away information that could be used against you. I believe that co-dependents often say too much in the hope that the "other" will then be drawn in to the close dependent relationship that they crave. Too often they simply come across as needy, or childish.

An A to Z of Co-Dependence

The other side of the coin is that if one does this with a similarly co-dependent person then you will be drawn to each other like moths to a flame. You will think that you have found your soul mate. Unfortunately this is probably not the case. What you have found is someone who thinks they can become dependent on you (because you obviously need them). You of course are seeking to do the same. Thus both of you are expecting to "take" from the relationship - and neither of you has a clue as to how to put anything back in! (Recipe for disaster #14a)

Watch yourself for dismissive statements, any automatic responses from childhood, any platitudes or clichés that indicate that you are not really engaging with the other person. In short - switch to manual override. Anyone who stays on autopilot will find himself back on the street sooner than you can say "co-dependent".

I have dropped every clanger ever built.

When my girl friend told me that she felt depressed, I cheerily said "Oh, you have nothing to worry about - there are millions of people much worse off than you". This would be a typical reaction from my parent's generation, thus I was pre-programmed to repeat it. What I was really saying, was that her feelings were either wrong or irrelevant. What might a more caring response have been? Suggestion: "I'm sorry to hear that. What has triggered that do you think?"

When she says something like: "My back is really hurting today". My response is again a pre-programmed "Oh dear".

I had not really taken in what she said, much less empathised with her pain. In fact I have simply dismissed her predicament - and carried on reading the paper….

The sub-text is that I don't really care about *her*. I only really care about getting *my* (co-dependent) needs met. I don't even care about my <u>real</u> needs.

If you want a <u>real</u> relationship you will just have to get <u>real</u>…

Platitudes to avoid:
1. Worse things happen at sea...
2. There's always someone worse off than you...

And avoid responding with a catalogue of your own problems...

Taking Care of Oneself - Not

This is what comes of being co-dependent. One is too aware of the (imagined) needs of others. The co-dependent has to be able to jump in to rescue or care-take at a moment's notice. His own needs are not monitored or recognised hardly at all.

So what gets neglected?

1. Personal care. Showering regularly, haircuts, dressing well, washing clothes, brushing of

teeth and hair, shaving. All get a highly perfunctory level of attention.

2. Career. I neglected to ever think about my career. I didn't bother to keep abreast of the latest technology and training, consequently I got left behind, and when made redundant found it impossible to get another job.

3. Relationships - I spread myself too thinly. The most important relationships got neglected and withered and died - time and time again.

4. Finances. These should have had more attention. I had been lucky to get into a well-paid industry. I never considered that the gravy train would ever end. It did of course.

5. The future. I was in denial that I would ever get old and need a pension. I would never get sick either - these things just would never happen to me.

6. Health. I only ever made half-hearted attempts to keep fit and take exercise. I nearly had to have new knees at the age of 50. I was lucky to get them back into reasonable shape. This was a wake-up call. I now know I need to do a certain level of exercise every day or I will be immobilised! (Literally and metaphorically)

Action: Make a list of the really important things, using the above list as a guide. And do them!

Thinking for others

See Assuming / Making Assumptions.

A good co-dependent will think he knows what others are thinking, and tell them what they are thinking or even feeling. This is usually quite irritating for the recipient of this information, as the co-dependent is usually totally incorrect.

The best approach when dealing with others is to just shut up and listen, if they are desiring to talk.If they are not being very talkative and you need to know how they are, then the best tactic must be to ask.

Trust

Growing up in a dysfunctional family can be tough. Whatever the issues are, the children will receive mixed messages and suffer from a lack of parental support at best. At worst there will be serious abuse and emotional and/or physical abandonment.

Almost invariably this will cause the child to have serious problems trusting adults, authority figures and likely problems forming relationships - whether that be with siblings, friends, work colleagues or life partners.

Trust is an integral part in forming relationships. Trust between two people is built slowly by personal interaction. Then comes friendship and then perhaps love - with an appropriate person. Trust in groups comes through working together. A person who cannot begin the trust process will remain forever an outsider - and be treated as "odd" and "difficult" by co-workers, for example. The person will feel that the world is against him, and feel justified in not trusting.

The damaged child will probably fail to transition into adulthood in a meaningful way, remaining forever in the grip of childhood programming. It is next to impossible for a person to break free of this behaviour by themselves.

The child's best hope is to have counselling and/or join twelve step programs such as Coda or Al-Anon. To get to that point the person's life will likely have been quite dysfunctional; experiencing divorce, addiction, abuse and possibly become an abuser.

Trusting a Co-dependent

One of the "Promises" of Co-dependents Anonymous (part of number 7) is "We learn to trust those who are trustworthy".

An A to Z of Co-Dependence

There may be two issues here. Co-dependents are often too trusting of others - showing little discernment about who we tell our secrets to, or worse, other's secrets. And our own predisposition to react dependently (childishly) to those we are with.

We don't consider that the information may be confidential, or that in fact it is just **not our business**. The child in us wants the attention and importance that having the information gives us.

It's not just about gossip either. My girlfriend said to me that because I was "So co-dependent" she "couldn't trust me". (Which I found confusing, because my self-image said that I was trustworthy - I had a lot to learn).

Because I found it so hard (impossible) to say "No" she couldn't rely on me to turn up on time. I would be trying so hard to please everyone, I would squeeze in as many "good deeds" as I could before setting off for our date - and sometimes arrive late as a result. These "good deeds" may have involved other women - even

149

ex wives and girlfriends - which didn't go down well either.

If you think that my girlfriend was being unreasonable about my behaviour you should get help with understanding this section - it is important. (See Relationships – Special ones)

Undermining Others

This can be a deliberate (unconscious) ploy by psychopaths and sociopaths. But we're not dealing with them here (just get the hell out of there!)

With all the best intentions, co-dependents do undermine others - with their advice giving, and showing others how it should be done. We are such experts - because we could never ask for help we have become experts at everything! (except what really matters - ourselves).

Young people particularly can become disempowered by parents eager to help their offspring. Sometimes we just have to let others make their own mistakes - even though it hurts us to see people struggle - people who need our help so much! When they ask for help we must be gracious and just suggest the minimum steps necessary to move them on a bit, then step back again - and try to contain our frustration.

See Controlling Others

Unavailability - Emotional

A good co-dependent watches out for any opportunity to Care-take or rescue *anyone* around. This, when acted upon will engender an emotional involvement with that person, and your partner, who is probably expecting some kind of exclusive relationship - may not get it! The co-dependent can be educated out of this mess.

The other case is where the unavailable person is an addict of some kind (any kind). Their emotions are tied up with their addiction, and thus they are significantly unavailable to you, their partner. This case appears to be to be almost completely intransigent. The addict must break free of his addiction.

In the former case however, the co-dependent needs to work hard on his recovery. Being threatened with the termination of the relationship may convince him to change. The addict however, will likely choose his addiction over the relationship.

Unmanageability

The reactive co-dependent has not usually thought things through to any extent. They have not really cared for their finances or their possessions. Often they have addictive or impulsive personalities.

Thus when something is offered to them that triggers their impulsivity or addictive nature they will spend money or do things that turn out later to have serious consequences. Things like not having enough money to pay the rent or other bills, like being incapacitated due to drink or drugs, and failing to turn up for work – and losing the job.

Being unable to hold down a job for long and / or indulging in drink or drugs can easily lead to loss of home, children taken into care and relationship breakdown, leaving that person to live on the streets. This is unmanageability in the extreme. It will get worse before it gets better. Get Help.

Valuing One's Labour - Not

An A to Z of Co-Dependence

As a co-dependent I would offer to help (any-one) and not ask for any payment. This is not the vegan (healthy) option!

- I was making people beholden to me, even trying to make them dependent on me (see taking a person's power)
- telling myself I wasn't worth anything
- making it hard for people to ask for help again
- making people feel uncomfortable
- making myself resentful - if they continued to take advantage of me

Problem;

- I don't know how to accept money or gifts gracefully
- I don't know what I'm worth
- I am not aware of my motives or;
- the effect on other people of my actions

Idea: I can accept gracefully, what people want to give me.

Victimhood

See also Drama Triangle.

Allowing oneself to slip into victim mode can be very tempting. As a victim the co-dependent is able to blame everyone else for their problems. They have thus absolved themselves of any responsibility for their lives.

Unfortunately this does not solve the problems, as no one else is actually to blame and no one else is responsible for their lives.

Some people thrive on being a victim. All kinds of ailments beset them, and they regale anyone within earshot of all the gory details. "Oh, poor you" they say, and the Victim thrives on the attention. The more esoteric the affliction the better.

One thing many people don't seem to notice is that the victim is never interested (not _really_ interested) in anyone else. They may say "oh, how are you?", or some other question, but they don't really listen to what anyone else says. They just want to get the conversation round to them. They will often talk over people if the talk is not about them.

Give them advice on how to manage their "condition" better - and they will have a hundred excuses why that won't work! They couldn't bear not to have the attention they get by having it.

It's not just ailments of course. Problems with children, spouse, work, neighbours etc. All are grist to the mill of life's victims.

The Victim's spouse and family however are often very different. They may well be sick and tired of the Victim's stance. And this is something else for the Victim to complain about! Yet more ammunition to get attention from any passing stranger (They're not fussy, they'll tell complete strangers the most intimate things).

It's not that there is nothing wrong with the victim. There is plenty wrong with them. The

NHS is bogged down with victims with real illnesses. The question is: What came first, the need to have the illness, or the illness? There is plenty of evidence that it is very often the former. Take away the need for the dis-ease and there is a miraculous cure!

The real problem appears to be attention seeking behaviour. The Victim can rarely have had the parent's attention during childhood. This has caused a pathological need for attention that can never be satisfied. Heavy duty counselling is prescribed! The Victim is "in Child" mode of course. They have probably hardly made any progress in the transition to adulthood.

If I don't sound exactly sympathetic to the plight of the victim, you could conclude that I may have been on the receiving end of the Victim's babbling at some point in my life. I may even have been a victim myself.

Vulnerability

An A to Z of Co-Dependence

Are you vulnerable? Are you easily taken in by get-rich-quick schemes? Are you easily alarmed by scam telephone calls purporting to be from the Inland Revenue? Do you fall for that advertisement offering this amazing new gadget by ordering it immediately? (When a quick search on eBay will reveal the same product at a much lower price) Some codependent recovery is obviously necessary.

On the other hand, do you seek out vulnerable people to take advantage of? Think of the phrase "13th stepping".

For the uninitiated this is occasionally observed in 12-step meetings, where a vulnerable newcomer is pounced upon, metaphorically speaking, by a more experienced person who finds them sexually attractive.

A mutual relapse is the common result. This is very serious, and obviously so in the case of substance abuse.

A codependent will seek out vulnerable people to be mutually dependent upon. This is not the route to a lasting and satisfying relationship.

Zoonotic Transference

This is not strictly speaking a co-dependent behaviour. It is in fact entirely fictional and non-existent! (to the best of my knowledge).

It is included here for the sake of completeness. I needed an entry under Z. Otherwise it would be an "A to V". If anyone has a better definition of this terrifying condition I will be pleased to include it! I am also in need of co-dependent behaviours beginning with W, X and Y.

I could have invented something silly to go under those headings, but one joke is enough. This is not meant to be a funny book. It's deadly serious.

Thanks for sticking with me!   Rob M

September 2021

Printed in Great Britain
by Amazon